Little People, **BIG DREAMS**®

RUTH BADER GINSBURG

Written by
Maria Isabel Sánchez Vegara

Illustrated by
Judit Orosz

Frances Lincoln
Children's Books

This is the story of a Jewish girl from New York called Ruth. Her mother was the bravest, strongest and most intelligent person she knew. She taught Ruth to be a lady, which meant being her own independent self.

The first step to being independent is to have a good education, something Ruth's mother never had. She was forced to drop out of school to help pay for her brother to go to university. But she had big plans for Ruth.

Sadly, just before Ruth graduated from high school, her beloved mother died. Ruth made a promise – she would do all the things her mum would have done if she had lived at a time when daughters were cherished as much as sons.

Ruth earned a scholarship at Cornell University, where she met another student called Martin. He was the first man she had ever known who cared that she had a brain. He became the love of her life and the one in charge of the kitchen.

They were partners, raising their family together while training to become lawyers. But not everyone saw women and men as equals

One day, a teacher accused Ruth and eight other women of each taking up a man's space... in a class of 550 students!

But Ruth had learned by heart the 14th Amendment of the Constitution, her country's highest law. She knew that it saw no difference based on gender. All people were equal citizens with equal rights.

She graduated from law school as one of the top students in her class and went to study in Sweden. Here, women were supported to develop their talents and succeed in their careers while raising their children.

Back home in the US, she became a professor and the leader of a feminist law group, working on groundbreaking cases to achieve equal rights for everyone. But feminism isn't just about girls, and Ruth's clients were not only women.

Ruth won hundreds of cases, and every tiny triumph was a big step towards equality. Before the Supreme Court, the highest court of all, she convinced the whole bench to apply the 14th Amendment to end gender discrimination.

Ruth had been a judge for years when the President asked her to join the Supreme Court. She was the second woman to ever sit on its benches. One of Ruth's major cases was against a military school that wouldn't allow female cadets to join.

Ruth persuaded all justices to get rid of that unfair rule. All but one: Antonin Scalia. He and Ruth disagreed, but they were still great friends. They admired each other's work – and they enjoyed going to the opera together, too!

Ruth was a grandma when she defended The Voting Rights Act, which said that no one should be denied the right to vote because of their skin colour. She lost that battle, but she gained the hearts of a new generation of law students!

After a long life fighting for equality, little Ruth became
all that her mother dreamed she could be, and more:

an inspiration for those who believe that by making fair and equal laws for everyone, we can transform people's lives.

RUTH BADER GINSBURG

(Born 1933 – Died 2020)

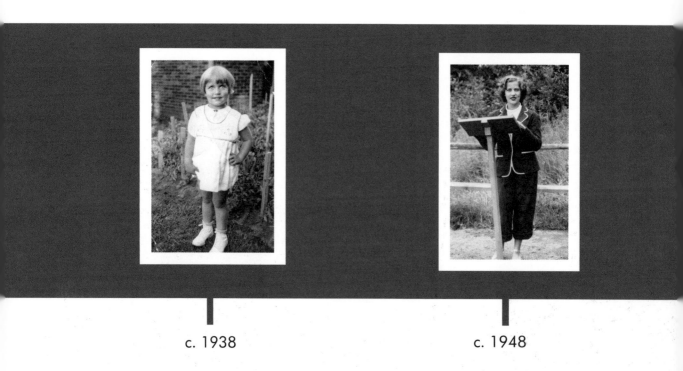

c. 1938   c. 1948

Joan Ruth Bader was born to an observant Jewish family in New York in 1933. Known as Ruth, she suffered tragedy early in her life – her only sister died at the age of six, and her mother died just before Ruth's high school graduation. Ruth was clever and talented. She earned top grades at school, and received a full scholarship to the prestigious Cornell University. It was there that she met Martin Ginsburg and they married in 1954. The couple both studied law while raising their family together. But although she was extremely qualified, Ruth struggled to find work, simply because she was a woman with children. When she visited Sweden in 1962 for a research project, Ruth was inspired by the country's advances towards gender equality – here she saw women receiving better healthcare

1977   2020

and more opportunities to work and study. In the 1970s, Ruth began
teaching and writing about equality, and as well as fighting for women's
rights, she argued for equality for male care-givers. She became a judge in
1980, and in 1993, she was appointed to the Supreme Court, the highest
court in the US. On its benches, she consistently ruled in favour of gender
equality, worker's rights and equal voting rights. Ruth became known for
her powerful disagreements with decisions made by the court, known as
'dissents'. However, she was good friends with many of her colleagues
despite their differences. Ruth continued in her role as a Supreme Court
judge until the end of her life in 2020. Her passionate defence of equality
made her a hero and a much-loved icon around the world.

Want to find out more about **Ruth Bader Ginsburg?**

Have a read of these great books:

I Dissent: Ruth Bader Ginsburg Makes Her Mark by Debbie Levy

The Story of Ruth Bader Ginsburg by Susan B. Katz

Brimming with creative inspiration, how-to projects, and useful information to enrich your everyday life, Quarto Knows is a favourite destination for those pursuing their interests and passions. Visit our site and dig deeper with our books into your area of interest: Quarto Creates, Quarto Cooks, Quarto Homes, Quarto Lives, Quarto Drives, Quarto Explores, Quarto Gifts, or Quarto Kids.

Text © 2021 Maria Isabel Sánchez Vegara. Illustrations © 2021 Judit Orosz.

Original concept of the series by Maria Isabel Sánchez Vegara, published by Alba Editorial, s.l.u

Little People Big Dreams and Pequeña&Grande are registered trademarks of Alba Editorial, s.l.u. for books, printed publications, e-books and audiobooks. Produced under licence from Alba Editorial, s.l.u.

First Published in the UK in 2021 by Frances Lincoln Children's Books, an imprint of The Quarto Group.

The Old Brewery, 6 Blundell Street, London N7 9BH, UK.

T (0)20 7700 6700 **www.QuartoKnows.com**

A catalogue record for this book is available from the British Library.

ISBN 978-0-7112-6468-7

Set in Futura BT.

Published by Katie Cotton • Designed by Karissa Santos

Edited by Katy Flint and Lucy Menzies • Production by Nikki Ingram

Editorial Assistance from Alex Hithersay

Manufactured in Guangdong, China CC062021

1 3 5 7 9 8 6 4 2

Photographic acknowledgements (pages 28-29, from left to right): 1. c. 1938 © Collection of the Supreme Court of the United States. 2. c. 1948 © Collection of the Supreme Court of the United States. 3. 1977 © Collection of the Supreme Court of the United States. 4. Ruth Bader Ginsburg is seen as she presents the Justice Ruth Bader Ginsburg Inaugural Woman of Leadership Award to Agnes Gund at The Library of Congress on February 14, 2020 in Washington, DC © Shannon Finney/Getty Images.

Collect the Little People, BIG DREAMS® series:

FRIDA KAHLO	COCO CHANEL	MAYA ANGELOU	AMELIA EARHART	AGATHA CHRISTIE	MARIE CURIE	ROSA PARKS

AUDREY HEPBURN	EMMELINE PANKHURST	ELLA FITZGERALD	ADA LOVELACE	JANE AUSTEN	GEORGIA O'KEEFFE	HARRIET TUBMAN

ANNE FRANK	MOTHER TERESA	JOSEPHINE BAKER	L. M. MONTGOMERY	JANE GOODALL	SIMONE DE BEAUVOIR	MUHAMMAD ALI

STEPHEN HAWKING	MARIA MONTESSORI	VIVIENNE WESTWOOD	MAHATMA GANDHI	DAVID BOWIE	WILMA RUDOLPH	DOLLY PARTON

BRUCE LEE	RUDOLF NUREYEV	ZAHA HADID	MARY SHELLEY	MARTIN LUTHER KING JR.	DAVID ATTENBOROUGH	ASTRID LINDGREN

EVONNE GOOLAGONG	BOB DYLAN	ALAN TURING	BILLIE JEAN KING	GRETA THUNBERG	JESSE OWENS	JEAN-MICHEL BASQUIAT

ARETHA FRANKLIN

CORAZON AQUINO

PELÉ

ERNEST SHACKLETON

STEVE JOBS

AYRTON SENNA

LOUISE BOURGEOIS

ELTON JOHN

JOHN LENNON

PRINCE

CHARLES DARWIN

CAPTAIN TOM MOORE

HANS CHRISTIAN ANDERSEN

STEVIE WONDER

MEGAN RAPINOE

MARY ANNING

MALALA YOUSAFZAI

ANDY WARHOL

RUPAUL

MICHELLE OBAMA

MINDY KALING

IRIS APFEL

ROSALIND FRANKLIN

RUTH BADER GINSBURG

MARILYN MONROE

KAMALA HARRIS

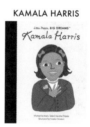

ALBERT EINSTEIN

ACTIVITY BOOKS

STICKER ACTIVITY BOOK

COLOURING BOOK

LITTLE ME, BIG DREAMS JOURNAL

Discover more about the series at www.littlepeoplebigdreams.com